Go On Lady, Do It!

Isobel M. Fyfe

Copyright © 2011 Isobel M. Fyfe
All rights reserved.
ISBN-13: 978-1463792701
ISBN-10: 1463792700

Dedication

To all the people in my poems, for poignant and treasured moments.

Table of Contents

In the still of the night 1
"Bloomin' 'eck" 2
Neil was neat 3
"A table is a table" 4
The water music rang loud and clear 5
The telephone rang and the doorbell rang 6
"Pain in the neck" 7
Humphrey was under the ivy 8
The depth of snow 9
Alastair stood at the window 10
"Is my hair right?" 11
The blue spotted feather 12
The Hoopoe 13
Papers 14
Funeral 15
'Pen the words' 16
Plan B 17
What a lovely tune he played that night 18
His mother and father had both gone away 19
"Goodbye, Alexandra" 20
Pescate 21
Hemel Hempstead 22
Appiano 23
The Hague 24
Germany 25
Sunday 26
Where are we going? 27
To Minnie 28
If it happened to me 29
We're not moving 30
Catnap 31
The lake is alive 32

The daylight slips	33
All in white	34
The sparrows that came for the cornflakes	35
In the courtyard	36
Nothing to do	37
"How are you this fine bright morning?"	38
Sharp and painful the stings	39
Stopping to touch snow	40
I didn't faint when I saw him	41
The first time I saw him	42
I rang the bell with trepidation	43
Early retirement	44
Routine is a cosy bed	45
Flight	46
The beggar	48
Airport	50
Crossroads	51
Waiting at the station	52
In the dark at dead of night	54
The hummingbird hawk-moth	55
Lost cat	56
Fly by night	57
France	58
Fireworks at Omegna	60
Cameron	61
Rainbow Ron	62
Happy birthday	64
Ariane's panda	65
The race	66
"Don't worry"	67
Joyce	68
Novelty	70
We walked on the back road from Auchinyell	71
Nothing was farther from my mind	72

50 years on 73
Fear and envy 74
There's no way I can pick you up 75
After it happened 76

Acknowledgements

Thanks to Flora for her technical expertise.

In the still of the night

In the still of the night
I can hear it snowing.
Snowflakes touch the window pane.
That's not rain,
It's snow.

Awake and curious
To prove myself right,
I brave the cold floor and peep out.
There's nought,
But snow.

"Bloomin' 'eck"

"Bloomin' 'eck," he said to his mum.
But he ran when she called his name.
"Why don't you be like him?" I said,
"And come when I call,
Not climbing the wall,
And playing at ball,
And shouting to all the other boys first?"
"I will come," he called,
"But I'd never say that to you Mum."

Neil was neat

Neil was neat,
Sat still on the seat,
Although he was only two.
In his Sunday best,
Like all the rest,
He waited in the pew.
When all was still,
In a voice that was shrill,
Said,
"Go on lady, do it!"
And a titter went round
The chapel that day,
As the little old lady
Started to play.

Isobel M. Fyfe

"A table is a table"

"A table is a table."
"Oh no, it's not.
It's a chair," he'd say
And he'd laugh a lot.

One day in town
To buy new shoes,
Harold stopped by a window
For time to choose.

"Not shoes," says baby,
Pointing in glee
"The boot's on the other foot,"
said he.

For Harold it was
Who taught him the game
Of giving things
Another name.

The water music rang loud and clear

The water music rang loud and clear
In the school assembly hall.
The children listened and waited
For the head to begin roll call.

"Tell me first the composer's name."
(They'd heard the tune before)
"I'll give you a hint. It begins with "H",
And you find it on every door.

Mid the forest of eager hands, he saw,
A little one, timid and shy.
"Yes, my dear, tell me," the kind head said,
And a hush fell to hear the reply.

"Hinge," said the tiny voice, right at the front,
And the head turned away with a grin.
As tears ran out under his glasses,
And rolled somewhere down under his chin.

Isobel M. Fyfe

The telephone rang and the doorbell rang

The telephone rang and the doorbell rang,
When Herbie was out for his run.
No one was left to watch him,
And suddenly, he was gone.

"The fire! Oh no, the fire!
He's jumped in the fire," said Jim.
And all that was left of the gerbil
Was a cinder growing dim.

"Pain in the neck"

"Pain in the neck," had a lovely ring.
So, "Pain in the neck," said she,
All the way from Cornwall to Cromer by the sea.
She bounced in the back,
Like a jumping jack.
Well, she was only three.
"What are you then?" said Dad in the front.
"Pain in the neck," said she.

Humphrey was under the ivy

Humphrey was under the ivy,
Taking the last of the sun.
Why didn't he come when I called him?
Tea time was over and done.

Why was that fly buzzing round him?
He's not moved his tail nor his head.
I ran down the steps from the kitchen,
And found that Humphrey was dead.

The depth of snow

No one could guess the depth of snow
That had fallen in the night.
We woke, we dressed, we got ready for school,
But something wasn't quite right.

It was all too quiet along our street.
"The road's blocked," shouted Miss Steed.
And a growing excitement filled our hearts,
For the work from which we'd been freed.

No work, no school, just clear the path,
And get ourselves down to the "Rose"
We had to get the local news,
Because one never knows.

One never knows one's neighbours
Till a crisis hits the town.
We were all one happy family
Snowed up at the Rose and Crown.

Isobel M. Fyfe

Alastair stood at the window

Alastair stood at the window,
The sky was really black.
"Oh my," said I, "Just look at the sky."
And the thunder gave a crack.

"Close the shutters. Let's go to the back."
Look out at the kitchen door:
The trees are bending right over the wall,
I can't see the field anymore.

"Close the door, the rain's coming in,
And the lightning's terribly bright.
And now the lights have all gone out.
Raise the shutter, we must have light."

Has a tree come down on the roof?
What's that horrible pounding sound?
Hailstones, driven like golf balls,
Are bouncing on the ground.

Go through the garden table,
Go through the garden chairs,
Branches, leaves and flowers,
Broken everywhere

Half hour has passed, and now at last,
The sun comes out again.
Forty years ago, they said,
It was the very same.

"Is my hair right?"

"Is my hair right?
Can you see auburn lights?"
"Well now, come here to the light."

"Is this skirt too tight?
Does it go with this shirt?"
"Well now, there's something not right."

"I might wear this belt,
Or tuck my shirt in.
Well now, does it make me look fat?"

"Have you got something else
You could put on instead?"
"Well now, I knew you'd say that."

Isobel M. Fyfe

The blue spotted feather

The blue spotted feather I found on the grass
Was all that was left behind,
When the young guinea fowl flew away from the farm,
For a life of a different kind.

Over the fence, through a gap in the trees,
And on to the road big and wide.
Into our garden for refuge he came,
Under the trees to hide.

No courage left, he'd made a mistake.
He wanted to get back in
To the safety of the farmyard pen,
And the others of his own kin.

His brothers united to cheer him on
And cackled and called in glee.
But it wasn't so easy to get back in
To the place where he longed to be.

The cackling and calling lasted a week.
Before he could find a way clear
They've all settled down at the farmyard now,
But the blue spotted feather is here.

The Hoopoe

One Saturday in April,
When the sky was dull and grey,
We were all a bit disgruntled
And had wasted most of the day.

We tried to think of useful ploys,
But a quarrel soon broke out.
And each one had stomped away to his lair,
When Mother gave a shout.

"Come quick and see this lovely bird."
They all pretend they haven't heard.
But sensing some urgency in the word,
Grudgingly, warily all appeared.

He was probing the grass for some morsel
With his long and firm straight beak,
A crest on his head, he was black, white and red.
"Shh! Don't anyone speak."

The hoopoe stayed some moments.
He'd come in search of food.
Did he know that these few moments
Would completely change our mood?

Papers

Papers rolling down the road,
Waved on by the tall dark tree,
Sand swirling up in orange clouds,
Dispersing like waves on the sea.

She's running down the dusty road.
But why? There's nothing there.
Men arrive in a smart blue car,
Lock up and run down the stair.

"Ten minutes," he said.
"I won't be long."
Ten minutes to capture a scene,
Or let it vanish forever,
As if it had never been.

Funeral

His funeral was in April,
A thousand miles away.
Eleven o'clock they said it would be.
How could we settle that day?
To do the normal things,
To talk and laugh and play?
It was a Saturday.

We gathered in the kitchen,
To drink a toast or two.
It seemed a fitting thing for us.
We didn't know what to do.
And then we planted pansies
Because we didn't know what to do.

'Pen the words'

I like the phrase,
'Pen the words.'
Do I separate them like cows and hens,
And feed them with memories and dreams?
In the happy pen go singing and Easter,
In the sad pen, grey and mistier.
In the warm pen, cosy and hug.
In the cold pen, money and mug.
Useless words like sitting and staring,
I mix with the dreams, not caring
To let empty words flow from my pen.

Plan B

What shall we do if it rains on the day?
We'll put into action Plan B.
But what shall we do if we fail the test,
Are second best and lose the quest?
Miss the train, or boat and plane?
Concede the game and carry the blame?
The answer's the same,
It's Plan B.

What a lovely tune he played that night

What a lovely tune he played that night.
"You'll like it," he said, and we did.
And now every time I hear that tune,
I remember the things we did.

We were all gathered round, the girls and the boys,
Talking about what we'd do
For the next five days of the Christmas break,
And sorting out who was who.

Emma was lively, and Ken was a rake.
Lisa was gentle, and Dave, goodness sake,
Wore the kilt and led each one a dance.
And for Gail it was all a romance.

We laughed, we played, we sang, we slept
We ate, we walked and we skied.
We took the best of all that there was,
Till the New Year came in with speed.

And sent us all our separate ways,
But memories linger long.
And we seem to be all together again,
Whenever I hear that song.

His mother and father had both gone away

His mother and father had both gone away,
When the babysitter brought him that day
To the school around eight forty-two.

But he didn't intend to stay, you could see,
By the way he frowned and looked daggers at me,
Then pointedly down at his shoe.

Come play in the house, or climb on the frame,
Take this new toy, or let's play a game.
Come on children. Please take his hand.

Get on the slide, or draw a tall tree,
Paint a green dragon, or cut out a three.
You can even play drums in the band.

All the suggestions were met with rebuff.
The sight of the school was more than enough
To set him a-punching and pounding.

With tight little fists he beat on the door.
He kicked at the tables and stamped on the floor,
Till down on his knees, he lay sobbing.

"Tweetie Pie's dead." I said in his ear.
"Where? Can I see? Is Tweetie Pie here?"
He replied to me all in one breath.

Filtered away the confusion and rage,
As he looked on the little bird, still in his cage.
He was rapt with the puzzle of death.

"Goodbye, Alexandra"

"Goodbye, Alexandra."
The children said.
And they sang songs
And ate up her cake.

"Can I play
With your toys?"
"Is it my turn to ride?"
"Can I have an egg
With a present inside?"

Time for home.
A battle ensues.
A melee of bags
And coats and shoes.

Everyone getting
ready to go.
Too busy to hear
Her plaintive, low,
"You'll never see me
again, you know."

Pescate

Spectacular mountains rise up from the lake.
I'm waiting and watching the scene
From a stone seat under a birch tree.
An old lady titivates in the garden
Of geranium pots, roses and hydrangeas,
With evergreen trees and variegated ivy.
Someone calls from within,
Birds call,
Traffic roars in the distance,
Then the church bells ring.
A door clicks open.
"Are you ready?" he calls.
"Not quite," I reply.
But I put on my shoes,
And go, all the same,
From this beautiful place.

Isobel M. Fyfe

Hemel Hempstead

Another beautiful place,
And I'm free to do what I want.
Blue and white sky,
Trees and bird songs,
And a wide open stretch of green, green grass.
Cool breezes rustle papers,
And turn the pages of the book
That I've rejected momentarily,
To savour this place as it is,
Now, today,
With the sun warm on my neck,
And the roar of traffic
A comfortable distance away.

Appiano

High up there,
Dark trees crowd round the white church,
And the vines cut wide green steps
Down the mountainside to the village
Of fountains and flowers,
Windows and shutters
Wide to the wall.

A cool breeze
Flutters the tablecloth's edge,
As I taste the wine,
Under a wide umbrella,
And watch the tourists with their children,
Laughing and talking,
Strolling and waiting
Expectantly for their pink and green ice cream.

The Hague

Don't move quickly,
Bend your head.
Your arm will take the weight.
You can write easily
For as long as you like
While the music plays.
Your legs ache no more,
Your feet touch the floor,
But there is no weight there.

Pictures from outside
Begin to appear.
All those leaves,
The colonial style houses
And the bright, clear
Windswept air.

I can feel the wind
On my face,
And round my eyes,
And not feel cold,
Because it's only an idea in my head.
The room is warm and quiet.
Hardly anything moves.

Is it always like this here?
For me, yes.
I want no change.
I've been away too long
And this music is like a lullaby,
With no crashing climax,
Just gentle, pleasing notes

Germany

A whole field of sunflowers was looking at us,
As we sped north that day,
In our camping van, with our cat's name on,
And the map spread to guide us the way.

Where were the deer we were promised?
Are those road signs really true?
Were the boulders all in that lorry we passed?
Or do they really fall out of the blue.

Is the lemon tree in the back of that car
Too cherished and precious to leave?
There's a cat on a lead in the car park.
Does it hanker to be on the move?

A small orange boat named "Garfield"
Is speeding south to the sun,
And horses are being transported with care,
So the drivers wave us on.

Are the lucky ones the people we pass,
Staying at home on the farm?
Or is their day spoilt by dreams of flight,
And escaping to somewhere warm?

Is the end of the road the best place to be?
Or should we stop somewhere along?
And take stock of all there is to enjoy,
And find where we really belong.

Sunday

There's no one here but us two.
We've dismantled the tree and swept all.
I've counted the cards and the letters,
Blacklisted those not on the wall.

It's a joke of course the blacklisting,
To put some fun to the day.
'Cos it's too quiet and awkwardly formal
When the family first goes away.

It's too easy to sleep on the sofa,
And ignore the same stuff on TV,
Or get lost in a book or a crossword,
Or eternally make cups of tea.

Let's look around for ideas,
For something constructive to do
To give us a new zest for living
And something to look forward to.

There's a catalogue here with smart cupboards
For keeping the house free of mess.
There are houses for sale in the mountains,
A dream I would like to express.

Let's walk out in the frost and the sunshine,
And there by the fields bare and wide,
A hundred and one different projects
Will be ours to discuss and decide.

It's the time of year for beginnings.
We really must get up and go.
Not wait for the more clement weather
For April comes sometimes with snow.

Where are we going?

Where are we going, for goodness sake,
Along the fast lane at high speed?
It's Saturday, don't you remember?
For timetables we have no need.

We've got to get to the lakeside,
To park and to savour the view.
That's why we're speeding along so fast,
To arrive before goodness knows who.

The furniture shop outing was different
The slow lane more than sufficed.
The driver yawned and dawdled
And digested the scenery twice.

"What's the time? Do they close in the lunch hour?"
"You're clutching at straws," I replied.
"They're open all day, from early till late"
"Do you think it'll be worth the ride?"

"Come on then. We'll go to the seaside.
Portofino our next port of call.
We'll look for some sprigs of mimosa.
The new cupboards can go to the wall.

Isobel M. Fyfe

To Minnie

Does it seem strange that you're eighty today?
Will you have a big cake for your tea?
Will you think of the things you did long ago?
And remember how things used to be.

Will you dream of the days in the country,
Out in the fields as a girl?
Or will you be thinking of more recent times
When we all came to Auchinyell

First great hugs in the lobby,
Then yellow fish for tea,
Raspberries for breakfast,
And long talks on the settee.

Memories can be wonderful,
As good as a film on TV.
But looking ahead's even better,
As we're never sure what we will see.

If it happened to me

If it happened to me
Would I be able to cope?
Would I sleep at night?
Would I languish and mope,
Languish and mope,
Languish and mope.

Would I tell all my friends,
And share out my woe?
Drain off their strength,
And watch them all go,
Watch them all go,
Watch them all go.

Would it be a secret,
To cunningly hide?
With smiles on the surface,
And torture inside,
Desolation inside,
Nothing inside.

Or could I accept it,
And still be the same
Deploying my strength
For playing the game,
And playing the game,
And playing the game.

Isobel M. Fyfe

We're not moving

We're not moving.
We're moving almost
At the speed of sound,
Creeping across
The mat of cloud,
Over the ground.
We've passed the high peaks,
With the snow and the tracks.
Whose tracks, you might wonder,
So high and removed from the towns?
Past the trees,
And rocks,
And far down below,
Straight roads,
That cut like a map,
The paper world
Into neat little shapes,
So that you can say,
 "Look, my house is here."

Catnap

I fell on the bed exhausted,
Duffy came and looked into my eye.
His whiskers tickled my nose and chin.
Did he fear I was going to die?

Soft pad on my cheek
Made me look up and smile.
Reassured, he turned away.
And massaging my body
With all four paws,
Found a comfy place to stay.

Weighty and warm, he lulled me to sleep,
Dreaming of nothing to do.
Then the telephone rang, and we both woke up.
I said, "Duffy, it's maybe for you."

Isobel M. Fyfe

The lake is alive

The lake is alive
With the afternoon breeze,
Shimmering, rippling,
Under the trees.

Lapping noisily
On to the shore.
Boats zoom by
With a deafening roar.

I sit and I think
Of the hill with the house,
Too perfect for words,
Just waiting for us.

No noise up there
But the cuckoo's call,
As we stood leaning
Over the wall.
And thinking how
We could foot the bill
Of the cost of that dream house
High on a hill.

The daylight slips

The daylight slips unnoticed away,
Some lamps are lit along the bay.
But we still see the water bright,
With shadows of boats and trees in the light.

A patch of sky is yet pale blue,
With a slice of moon and a star or two,
To remind us that the day's near done.
Now all the far side lamps come on.

Reflections, deep, long stripes reach down
Into the lake below the town
Colours, orange, blue and white,
Skim the black water, and it's night.

Isobel M. Fyfe

All in white

All in white
For the summer heat,
Jim's reading a book
In the garden seat.
No flicker, no stir
From the umbrella fringe.
The garden is still,
And the paling's turned orange.

A swallow swoops by,
Low over the wall.
The chaffinch has finished
His evening call.
Cats loll on the pavement,
Last warm place to browse.
The coolness and darkness
Arrive unannounced.
Jim closes his book
And comes into the house.

The sparrows that came for the cornflakes

The sparrows that came for the cornflakes
Wore a hundred shades of brown.
All speckles, stripes and patches,
Different, each one that flew down.

We had plenty of time to watch them.
Seemed like wives at a market stall.
Could they really be all that hungry?
Or was it the fun of the free for all?

When they swept away in a flurry
To bargain hunt elsewhere,
A late one arrived expectantly,
But no crumb was left to spare.

My hand reached out for a biscuit,
But he flew off in a fright.
So the poor little bird got nothing.
His timing wasn't quite right.

How many times does it happen?
We wait, or impatient move on,
Making our own decisions,
And gain or lose a crumb.

Isobel M. Fyfe

In the courtyard

We sat in the courtyard after our swim,
Hilda, Jill and I.
Like a private room, it seemed to be,
Yet open to the sky.

Young boys' voices out in the street,
And music from further away,
Enhanced the stillness of the place,
As the wall caught the sun's last ray.

No footsteps rang on the cobbles,
Where small weeds traced each row.
No movement came from the towering spruce,
As the bats slid to and fro.

We talked in quiet voices,
Sensing the peace and the calm,
That made the evening so special,
To recall in years to come.

Nothing to do

Nothing to do this afternoon.
I've finished the business in town.
I'm refreshed from a shower and a long cool drink,
What luxury, just to lie down.

What's on the news, the state of the pound,
An earthquake near Japan,
Campers alarmed by a venomous cloud.
Sleek yachts elude the tax man.

What's this to me? I'm on holiday.
There'll be someone else on the spot
With youth and brains and energy,
The knowhow, the technique, the lot.

Just waiting for such opportunities,
To jump in and have a say.
And promote some cherished project,
But not me, not now, not today,

"How are you this fine bright morning?"

"How are you this fine bright morning?"
"Fine and bright," he cried.

"How are you this-----?"
"Terrible," he sighed.

Was it worth it, all that shouting,
Celebrating and carrying on?
Just one more dance,
Just one more song.

"Do you want coffee?"
"Hard question. Don't speak."
"Do you want coffee?"
Response very weak.

"What's going on here?
Is everyone up?
Why didn't you wake me?
At least pass me a cup.
A cup of life giving tea."

Sharp and painful the stings

Sharp and painful the stings,
On hands and plimsolled feet
Chestnuts, pressed out from their cushions of spines
Are harvested complete.

Their ample, glossy roundness,
Makes atonement from the harm
From all their spiky, prickly coats,
Sweet chestnuts soothe the palm.

Smells waft warm and woody
From the pan upon the hearth.
Stinging, burning fingers put
Mealy crumbles into the mouth.

Delicious, mealy crumbles,
You'll want to taste again,
Delicious, nutty autumn flavour,
Fruits of sun and rain.

Isobel M. Fyfe

Stopping to touch snow

Stopping to touch snow,
Sifting dry crystals,
Hand height by the roadside.

Stopping to wipe tears,
Warm tears from the brightness
Of snow by the roadside.

Stopping to read
Of the boy long ago,
Just seventeen years old,
Who died by the roadside.

Stopping to look
For the tiny green siskin,
Piping a tune in a tree
By the roadside.

Stopping to listen
To small stones
On the move
Down to the roadside.

Stop to test ice,
And gingerly slide,
And stamp till it cracks
By the roadside.

Stop to look back,
To see how far we've come,
And view our new house
From the roadside.

Pick up a fir cone,
And carry it home.
Set it free from its rut
By the roadside.

I didn't faint when I saw him

I didn't faint when I saw him,
In bandages, asleep.
It wasn't my son who'd pushed him,
And put his gas down to a peep.

I didn't shed tears at his bedside,
Or add to the general furore.
I wasn't the culprit's father
Apologising for the score.

I was only the teacher,
Who lay awake at night.
Had I been more vigilant,
Would things have been alright?

Could I have known what would happen?
Foreseen how things might be?
And instead of Hurricane Harry,
Wasn't the culprit really me?

Isobel M. Fyfe

The first time I saw him

The first time I saw him,
He hugged me too much,
And my heart sank within me.
He clung to my hand,
And my dress, and his touch,
Left me cool, distant and wary.

What had I done
To warrant this show
Of boisterous affection?
I looked at his eyes,
But his gaze was a blank,
And between us no real connection.

He staggered on by
With ungainly walk,
No particular goal in mind.
He ground his teeth
And wouldn't talk,
But chewed all he could find.

"The doctors say
There's nothing wrong.
Just retarded a little," mum said.
With her heart full of love,
And a desperate hope
That one day he'd be forging ahead.

I rang the bell with trepidation

I rang the bell with trepidation,
Unprepared for her salutation,
I didn't have an invitation.

"Come in. I'm fine."
"You're looking well."
To see her there, you'd never tell.
Her face aglow, she was looking swell.

The children ran freely out and in,
As she told of the battle she might not win,
Voicing her fears with a rueful grin.

But she didn't look me in the eye.
We were both afraid that we might cry,
As she talked things out with never a sigh.

"Thank you for coming. You've brightened my day."
She said to me as I went away,
Past the children, politely stopping their play.

How can she cope, faced with such fear?
To leave husband and children alone and drear.
Will she live to see another year?

Early retirement

Nothing dirty,
Nothing dusty,
Nothing untidy, no drawers all jumbly.
No piles of papers or books all asundry.
No clothes on the bed, on the floor, on the door,
No toothpaste on mirrors, no stains on the floor.
No need to shop, the cupboards are full.
At five minutes warning, we'll feed a whole school,
But nobody comes, they're all working.
We've time to kill,
But we're jumping the gun.
Clothes and shoes queue up to be worn.
Not that there's anything pending the morn
To warrant a dress rehearsal.

Days to fill,
We sit in the sun,
No rush, no tear or tasks to be done
By impossible deadlines, and again to press on.
It's suddenly a complete reversal.

I'm losing the thread,
Time is slipping away
I'm spinning out chores till they last all day
A web to entrap me. A ruse to delay
Having to think of a worthwhile pursuit,
A work of my own that would bear me fruit.
Will I find the right purpose to give me the zest
To practise the things I know I do best?
I don't know. I've just been home a week.

Routine is a cosy bed

Routine is a cosy bed.
I'm safe in my routine.
No indecision wracks my brain,
I fantasize and dream.

And if that dream should lure me up
To climb life's spiral stair,
Routine is the handrail
That helps to get me there.

There are routine sounds to comfort me
When I am all alone.
The swish of tyres along the road,
And you are coming home.

The outline of the mountain peaks
Obscures the sun's last ray.
This, the routine sight that greets me
When I've been away.

Routine smells have meaning
Through the seasons of the year.
Hint of mothballs in the metro
Tell us change is in the air.

Routine is a circle
That smaller, smaller grows.
Or wider, ever wider yet.
It's up to me to choose.

Flight

Their flight was at 3.20.
At ten she'd on her hat.
He wore his dark green jacket.
Cases and bags were packed.

Kisses, hugs,
Pats on the back,
Holding hands,
Distance starts,
Waving arms,
Blowing kisses,
Beep of the car,
The gap is wide.
Tears are falling,
Gasping, sobbing,
Torn apart,
The miles divide.

The house now quiet and empty.
We've lots of work to do.
The therapeutic qualities
Help to see us through.

Distant murmur,
A plane in the sky.
Right time right flag
They're so close by.
We're waving arms,
Blowing kisses,
Drone of the engines,
The gap is wide.
They're disappearing
Over the mountain,
Vapour trails,
The miles divide.

Go On Lady, Do It!

Ridiculous joy and elation
Such contact gave to us
Ridiculous joy and elation,
When they said they'd seen our house.

Isobel M. Fyfe

The beggar

Why would
He do it?
How could
He do it?
Too smart
By far.
Too neat,
Too clean.
Too young,
Too lean.
Altogether too
Good looking.

Blue jeans,
Blue jacket,
Two sticks
And one leg.
He stood there,
Hand held out
To the crowd.
Not too proud.
And a lump
Came to my throat,
As I passed him
A note.

Go On Lady, Do It!

Eyes met
And a rush
Of thanks,
Profuse thanks,
Too much
For too little,
Waved me
On and away,
Out of my depth
I hurried.
Too shy
To ask.

Isobel M. Fyfe

Airport

Dark hair, light hair,
They moved through the crowd.

Dark hair, light hair,
They waited in the queue.

Dark hair, light hair,
They stood at the desk.

Dark hair, light hair,
They turned and came to me.

Dark hug, light hug,
Time for us to part.

Dark hair, light hair,
Last wave and they are gone.

Crossroads

I sat by the bar and watched him.
He'd be all of seven years old, I thought.
Blond tousled hair and dark brown eyes,
Bright yellow jacket, luminous,
Like a mustard field in June.

He stood in admiration,
Of the teenage boys at the slot machine.
Did he hope one day to be one of them,
With friends, the gear, the stance,
With money to spend as he liked?

In the street I waited.
There he goes again, I thought.
Running and dodging between parked cars.
And waving aloft a note,
He scurried into the bar.

Out, radiant, beaming, grinning,
Huge sandwich in his hand. He showed
It to the lady at the bus stop.
She wasn't his mum. His mum
Had the baby on her back.

.And watched him as he ate
Then warmed, he shrugged the jacket off.
He smiled, and fondly touched her shoulder
And set to work again,
Begging at the traffic lights.

Isobel M. Fyfe

Waiting at the station

Waiting at the station,
I saw her sitting there,
Bright headscarf, dull face, worn coat,
Not going anywhere.

Waiting in the station,
A bench on which to cling,
Warm at least, and dry
Not expecting anything.

A playground for her children,
Free to run about
Within the invisible boundary,
By custom measured out.

As far as passport photos,
A cubicle of fun.
A flimsy, swinging curtain
Hid the little one.

Her brother came to find her,
And rained blows to her head,
Saw my disapproval,
And defiantly he said

"I can easily smack her."
And then made his demand
For money, a coin or two,
That I might have at hand.

My hand was not forthcoming.
My look was not for him.
My sympathy for the victim,
Of his every nasty whim.

Go On Lady, Do It!

With childish intuition,
His outstretched hand slunk back.
At once he knew he'd lost his cause
By that impetuous smack.

Waiting in the station,
She saw the interchange.
Bright headscarf, dull face, worn coat,
She saw nothing strange.

Isobel M. Fyfe

In the dark at dead of night

They stood at the wall and waited,
In the dark at dead of night,
The air from the wood rose up so chill,
Still they lingered, nothing in sight.

Then came the shuffling and rustling.
Would he really be run to earth,
All unconcerned and unknowing?
They waited with baited breath.

But the rustling faded to silence.
Weary watchers dwindled away.
Then a light came on, and a shout rang out.
"I've seen him. He went down that way."

A smile on his face as he said it,
Beaming from ear to ear,
All for the sight of a badger,
This tension and moment of cheer.

The hummingbird hawk-moth

Such a refined insect,
The hummingbird hawk-moth.
He comes in the morning,
Again in the evening,
More hummingbird than hawk-moth.

No trampling on petals,
No bending of leaves.
Disturbing no flower stalks,
Hovering and flitting,
His baton at the ready
Like the conductor scans
His orchestra, the flowers,
Vying for attention,
To play their part on cue.
Powerless alone, wait
For him to expedite
His purpose with precision.
Invisible wings
Thrum vibrant music.

Until one August morning,
I find him on the ground,
All chalky winged and stiff,
More hawk-moth than hummingbird.

Lost cat

She didn't come to meet me
When I came home that day,
And I wondered what had kept her.
She was never far away.

She didn't come to twine my legs,
As she had done before,
Then bound across the flower bed
To beat me to the door.

I opened up the empty house,
I searched the garden bare.
I called and waited, breath abated,
Nothing stirred the air.

I asked the friendly neighbours,
And looked fearfully down the road.
No inert furry bundle there,
For that much I was glad.

We searched the lanes and woodlands
And the gardens all around.
But no one had seen Snooky,
And she was never found.

Fly by night

We watched the game with bated breath,
Came home exultant and tired to death.
Fell into bed and shut my eye,
"Oh no, my god, there's this one fly."

The one -swipe fly swat close at hand,
I sit up in bed and where does it land?
Right on the hand that holds the swat.
What can you do? I know not what.

Let him escape for one more time.
He's sure to land within my aim.
He's nowhere and my eyes are closed
I pull up the sheet to rest reposed.

Or do I? I think, will it land on my nose?
It's so hot here, dare I my shoulders expose?
I lie there stiff, I'm all on edge,
Ready to leap, the swat's on the ledge.

And even though it's total calm,
I'm listening, awaiting that buzzing alarm.
Till sleep comes quietly and all is repose,
And I couldn't care less should it land on my nose.

Isobel M. Fyfe

France

The sun shone in the morning.
We didn't wait to think.
We plunged into the swimming pool,
We thought that we were really cool,
No shivering on the brink.

We played at being ferries,
From Dover and Calais.
The swallows swooped in graceful dives,
In hope of catching many flies
To see them through the day.

Breakfast was baguettes,
Pain chocolat and croissants,
Under the shady lime tree.
From the lady at the boulangerie,
We knew all the local haunts.

The redstart in the woodshed
Flitted to and fro.
The cuckoo called from a long way away,
The ring doves cooed to have their say,
And we talked about where we'd go.

A market at Marcigny,
A picnic by the Loire,
Swings in a park with a great lake view,
A visit to the shops at Charlieu,
Each day we'd venture far.

Lunch was entertaining,
With stories round the table,
Of the wide mouthed frog or aliens in bed.
I never got the punch line said
For laughing left me incapable.

Go On Lady, Do It!

Evening, we'd climb to the orchard
And feast on cherries red.
Barbeque smoke would waft great smells.
We'd eat our fill of frogs and snails,
Then the children would go to bed.

Candlelight on the table,
We'd sit and sip some wine.
"Night, night," we'd call to the children inside.
"Night, night," the sleepy voices replied.
And over us stars would shine.

Fireworks at Omegna

People selling, some are buying,
Sweets for eating, beer for drinking,
Games for playing, lanes for strolling.
All come to a standstill.

Wafts down an invisible thread,
Drawing the loosely woven crowd
Into a tight mat round the lake,
Waiting for the signal.

A treble voice, a cry of laughter,
Ring clear above the throng's low murmuring.
Lake sounds of the water lapping,
And the expected signal comes.

Ear-splitting, thundering, booming, resounding,
Clean through each body and back from the mountain.
We're caught in vibrations, elation and thrill.
Each one in his own way responding.

Tears of emotion fall with the stars
Cascading around us and yet stopping short.
Fountains of light leap up from the lake,
Bright candles, like swans gently floating.

Final flurries of sparks, and sounds die away.
Like a wave on the shore, the crowd breaks away
Disperses, unwinds from the grasp of the show.
The summer vacation ends here.

Cameron

He called me from his bedroom
In the middle of the night,
And together we looked at Orion's stars,
Then he slept till morning light.

He called me at the break of day,
The sun still pale and low,
And together we watched pink clouds race by,
The church spire, trees and a crow.

He called me from his playroom
To buy things from his shop.
A pile of cars were ice creams
And the train a bottle of pop.

He called me from the playground
To sit down and have a chat.
But it was all a trick to start
A chasing game of tat.

He called me from the garden
To show me to his friends.
And I met a row of tractors
With Patrick, Charlie and Ben.

He called me to come dancing
When he heard them play my tune.
It was only "Something Stupid"
But we skipped around the room.

He called me from a long way off
To say he'd come to stay.
And the bells ring out at Boleto
To celebrate the day.

Isobel M. Fyfe

Rainbow Ron

Once there was a parrot.
They called him Rainbow Ron.
He wasn't as green as others seem,
Their colours he outshone.

He'd flown off to Malaysia,
And come back starry eyed.
Then all the way to Scotland,
For tartan wings and plaid.

Then tired of all the travelling,
And sitting on a perch,
He thought he'd like a real chair,
And so began his search.

He flew down over Ashtead,
And looked into the school,
He saw the parrot classroom,
Of little chairs t'was full.

One chair in particular
Almost had his name,
Even his favourite tartan,
Excited, in he came.

The teacher said, "No talking".
Which was hard for the poor bird.
So instead of sitting squawking,
He listened to every word.

And later on, the children gone,
Running home to tea,
Rainbow Ron recited all
The lessons with great glee.

Go On Lady, Do It!

Squawking here and squawking there
"Two and one make three".
Loving learning lessons
On a chair called CameRon Lee.

Isobel M. Fyfe

Happy birthday

Along came Allosaurus
Saying, "What's the date today?"
Tyrannosaurus did reply,
"It'll be Cameron Lee's birthday
Only two hundred million years from now.
We'd better send a card
To wish him Happy Birthday."
And they clomped around the sward.

Iguanodon, triceratops,
How can we send our greetings
Two hundred million years away.
They hurried to their meeting.

Up spoke snake and turtle,
"We can all live on,
To take your loving message."
"Wait," said Amebelodon.

"What about the lizards,
They'll live in Boleto
In Nanpa and Nanma's garden,
They'll take him a libretto."

So here it is,
With love and hugs,
From all us creatures here,
Past, present and future,
To wish you a wonderful year.

Ariane's panda

A panda came from China
Along the silk road,
Looking for some bamboo shoots.
They were his favourite food.

He journeyed through the desert.
He came to Samarkand.
By then, of course, he realised
Things had got out of hand.

He couldn't read the road signs.
He was lost and far away.
How he ended up in Ashtead,
No one can ever say.

Heard mention of a panda class.
"Why, that's just what I need
To get me back to China,
I have to learn to read."

So he came to lessons,
And practised every day,
Till he could read from any book.
"Now I can go away."

"Don't go away," cried Ariane.
"Stay and play with me.
I have bamboo in my garden,
So you can come to tea."

And so he stayed another day,
But the call of Kublai Khan
Was in his little panda heart.
"Come to see me when you can."

Isobel M. Fyfe

The race

She looked like me, and he looked like you.
About the same age, they were running.
Both smartly dressed in their Sunday best,
As if for a pleasant day's outing.
Short panicky steps and gasping for breath,
No quick sprint for a bus to go shopping.
T'was a race for their lives across a wide bridge,
And behind them people were gunning.
Of all the war scenes that I've viewed in the past,
This to my mind keeps recurring,
Because she looked like me, and he looked like you,
And behind them people were gunning.

"Don't worry"

"Don't worry," she said.
And she kissed his head
As he lay in bed,
While around them all hell had broke loose.

Injured in war,
Bewildered and sore,
She'd carried him far.
They were stunned to survive such abuse.

"Which bullet, and who
Could do this to you?
My son, if you knew,
Would you tell him it's time for a truce?"

But the enemy comes,
And brings us his bombs,
To shatter our homes.
And to flee or to stay we must choose.

No relief to surrender,
No mercy, just plunder,
The village asunder,
While the whole world awaits the bad news.

Joyce

We met at the corner
And walked to school,
That's how we became friends.

We'd wait for each other
And take the same tram,
Or look in the shops
And walk all the way home.
That's how we became friends.

We ate our sweets
At the exact same speed,
That's why we became bosom pals.
We'd see a sad film
And together we'd sob,
We'd find each other
In the midst of a mob,
That's why we became bosom pals.

We'd laugh till our faces
Were wet with tears.
We'd torture ourselves,
Expressing our fears.
What if our mothers should suddenly die?
It happened to someone we knew, by the by.
That's how we became bosom pals.

We'd organise parties and invite all the boys
And girls in our class and make lots of noise.
We'd tell our adventures of Saturday night,
Mid gasps of amazement and shrieks of delight,
Because we were bosom pals.

Go On Lady, Do It!

Some years have passed by
And we've each gone our ways,
But it's easy for us
To recapture those days.
It seems we'll be friends for life.

Isobel M. Fyfe

Novelty

In the days when everyone darned their clothes,
And a novelty item was spam,
We'd acquired a taste for sugarless tea,
While Mother made toffee and jam.

We were wrapping the toffee to give to our friends
At the Christmas party next day,
When mother returned from a shopping spree.
You could tell she had something to say.

What if she'd got us some really fresh eggs?
Or syrup to put on the bread?
Tinned peaches even, no couldn't be that.
"Look a packet of straws," she said.

Drinking straws for the lemonade.
Such a thing we'd have never divined.
And the fact that it gave us such pleasure,
Has always lived on in my mind.

We walked on the back road from Auchinyell

We walked on the back road from Auchinyell,
In the clear, cool autumn air.
The fields were bare, the last leaves fell,
And our hearts were in despair.

No work, no money, and bills to pay.
A recipe for doom.
Ahead we feared that problems lay,
Lurking in the gloom.

Instead, ahead, a big turnip had rolled,
And lay at the kerbside green.
Awaiting rescue from the cold,
To fill our soup tureen.

But foolish pride said, "Hang about,
Till all the people have gone."
So we loitered, and they, in passing shout,
"Wow a turnip!" and carried it home.

Isobel M. Fyfe

Nothing was farther from my mind

Nothing was farther from my mind,
Than that the fierce, cold, biting wind
Could whip the ice cream from my hand

Memories, long distant past,
Borne along each bracing blast,
Surged in and under a sky o'ercast.

Away as far as the eye can see,
A strip of sand and sun on the sea,
Mind fine summer days at Balmedie.

I've gathered stones of granite grey.
Will it matter that they're taken away
For souvenirs of a bygone day.

Were these stones here when I played on the sand,
Got tossed by a wave and thought, "This is the end---?
Now fifty years on I'm back where I stand.

I feel the presence of Jim at the fence,
As together we gaze at this vast expanse,
In time, in place and circumstance.

A grand old lady has passed away.
A mother, a granny till yesterday.
Shaping a landmark along life's way.

50 years on

I walked around the shopping mall
With an hour or two to spare,
Before our big reunion,
Wondering who'd be there.

I watched for likely people.
Could she be one of them?
But when I arrived at the old school pub,
Saw none within my ken.

A group there was withstanding,
And I gingerly climbed the stair.
"You must be Izzy Gauld," they said.
"We knew you by your hair."

I drew a blank but brazened it out,
And asked them who was who.
Then suddenly it all came clear,
Like an answer to a clue.

Name tags issued, soon discarded.
We were soon at one.
The hazards of our schooldays
Were, in retrospect, such fun.

Gone the fears and worries
That haunt us in our youth,
In front of our contemporaries,
Afraid to speak the truth.

We had no proud pretensions,
All competition done.
Age had put us at our ease,
The battle had been won.

Fear and envy

Why is it when you're far away,
Everyone's loved ones are there to stay,
And visit them, phone them every day
Eat with them, meet with them by the way.

Why is it when your child is ill,
All the kids are playing down the hill,
Laughing and shouting with voices shrill,
And only your house is quiet and still.

Why is it when we haven't heard,
That you're safely home from your travels abroad.
Trains crash, planes explode, buses run off the road
Into ravines till we hear your word.

Why is it when we slave and still have no money,
People are shopping and spending, it's irony,
To think that they're all flying off to holidays sunny,
And buying new cars, while we watch every penny.

Why when we're together and times are good,
With the envy of all around us accrued,
Do we fear to offend them with our mood,
Of everything being as it should.

There's no way I can pick you up

There's no way I can pick you up
From your depths of dark despair.
From where I stand, it's a passing cloud,
But you're in there and I care.

I care too much and press home the point.
The point is too painful to bear.
And I realise, the last thing you want,
Is a clearing of the air.

So I wait for you to be ready.
To rise above the grey,
And dark voluminous cloud,
That's hiding this wonderful day.

Isobel M. Fyfe

After it happened

After it happened, I didn't want
The tulips to burst into bloom,
Nor azaleas and wisteria,
They must wait till you come home.

I didn't want the grass to grow,
The spring flowers nearly gone.
The cuckoo called, "Too soon, too soon,"
'Cos you are not yet home

I didn't want to buy new clothes.
In case you knew me not.
But in the green hospital apron,
I was covered head to foot.

Do you hear the stories I tell you now
Of the things that we did once?
Do you remember the songs I sing?
Although you make no response.

Do you see the tears that fall?
Is that why you close your eyes?
Or stare at a point on the ceiling
When I have to say goodbye?

About the Author

Isobel Fyfe was born in Aberdeen, Scotland and taught in Scotland, England and Italy. She has a daughter, two sons and four grandchildren. She is now retired.

> *Every now and then*
> *Somewhere along the way*
> *I stop and say*
> *Go on lady, do it!*

Made in the USA
Charleston, SC
26 November 2011